W9-BMP-193

First American Edition 1994 by Kane/Miller Book Publishers
La Jolla, California

Originally published in Japan under the title Onara (A Story of
Farts) by Fukuinkan Shoten, Publishers Inc, Tokyo, 1978

Copyright © 1978 Shinta Cho
American text copyright © 1994 Kane/Miller Book Publishers

All rights reserved. For information contact:
Kane/Miller Book Publishers
P.O. Box 8515, La Jolla, CA 92038-8515

First American Paperback Edition, 2001

Library of Congress Cataloging-in-Publication Data

Cho, Shinta, 1927-
[Onara. English]
The gas we pass : the story of farts / by Shinta Cho :
translated by Amanda Mayer Stinchecum. – 1st American ed.

1. Flatulence-Juvenile literature. [1. Flatulence.] I. Title
RC862.F55C48 1994   94-14267
612.3-dc20
ISBN 0-916291-52-9
ISBN 1-929132-15-8 (pbk.)

Printed and bound in Singapore by Tien Wah Press Pte. Ltd.
1 2 3 4 5 6 7 8 9 10

THE GAS WE PASS

The Story of Farts

By Shinta Cho

Translated by Amanda Mayer Stinchecum

A CURIOUS NELL BOOK

Kane/Miller BOOK PUBLISHERS

When an elephant farts, the farts are really big.

People fart too.

Bubbles rise . . . plip, plip, plip.

When you eat or drink, you swallow air.

And if you eat or drink in a big hurry,
you swallow a whole lot of air.

The air that escapes through your mouth becomes a burp.

When it comes out the hole in your bottom, it's a fart, also called passing gas.

THE PATH OF AIR AND FOOD

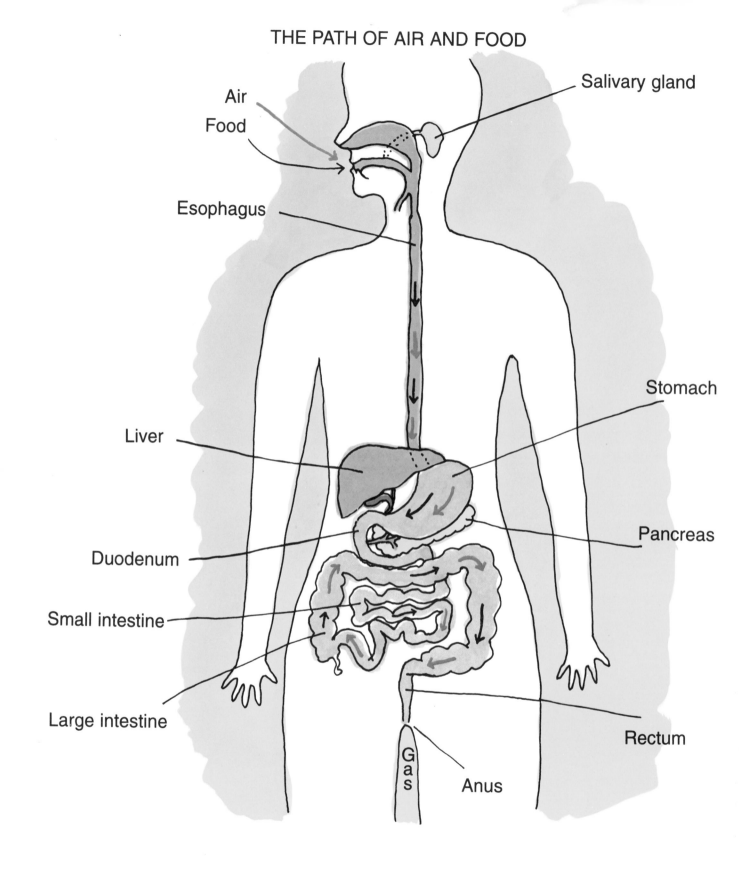

Air

Food

Salivary gland

Esophagus

Stomach

Liver

Duodenum

Pancreas

Small intestine

Large intestine

Rectum

Gas

Anus

Besides coming from the air you swallow, farts come from the gases found in your large intestine. These gases are made when leftover food (food that your body doesn't use) is broken down by bacteria, rots and becomes poop.

That's why farts stink!

Large intestine
↓

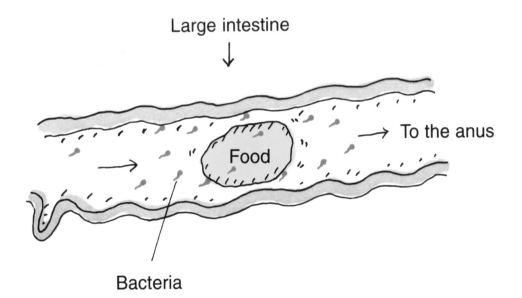

Food

→ To the anus

Bacteria

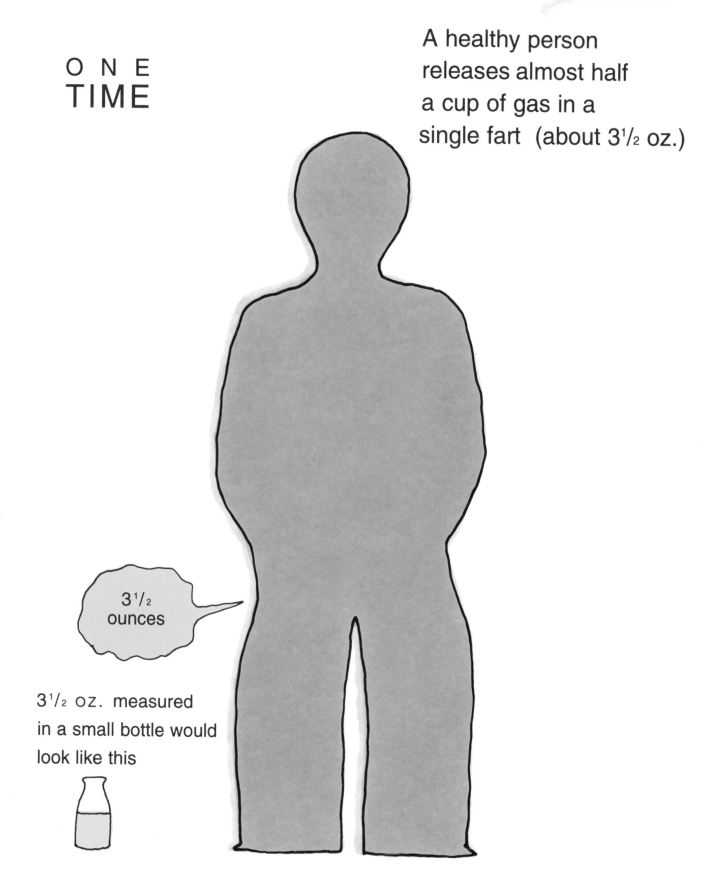

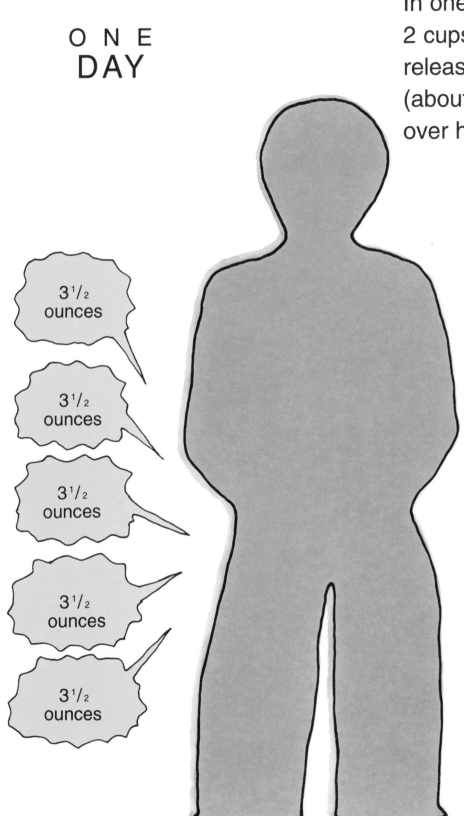

If you try too hard to hold your farts,
your stomach may hurt,
you could get dizzy or you could
get a headache.

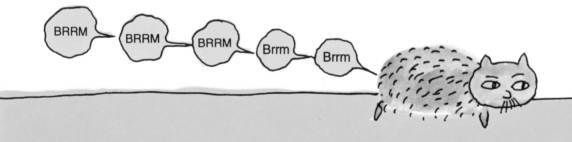

So, don't hold them in—pass that gas!

When you begin to fart after an operation,

it means your intestines have started working again.

Some farts smell bad, and some don't.
When you fart after eating meat, fish, eggs or
things like that, your farts smell really bad.

When you fart after eating sweet potatoes or beans, however, they don't smell very much at all.

That's why the farts of animals that eat meat smell so terrible.

The farts of animals who eat things like potatoes and grass—
such as elephants, rhinos and hippos—
don't smell that bad.

But eating potatoes or grass causes lots of gas to
build up in their intestines which makes them fart a lot.

Animals such as skunks and stink bugs protect themselves by letting out a smelly fluid from near the holes in their bottoms.

This is not farting.

Skunk

Stink bug

And that's the story of farts.

MY BODY SCIENCE

★ SERIES ★

All About Scabs

Breasts

Contemplating Your Bellybutton

Everyone Poops

The Gas We Pass (The Story of Farts)

The Holes In Your Nose

The Soles of Your Feet

Todos Hacemos Caca